ARTIST
TRANSCRIPTIONS
PIANO

THE CEDAR WALTON COLLECTION

Cover Photo: Danny Miller

ISBN 0-7935-4853-5

HAL•LEONARD®
CORPORATION

7777 W. BLUEMOUND RD. P.O. BOX 13819 MILWAUKEE, WI 53213

Visit Hal Leonard Online at
www.halleonard.com

THE CEDAR WALTON COLLECTION

CONTENTS

BIOGRAPHY

Cedar Anthony Walton Jr. has been known for years as one of a handful of masterful accompanists in bop and hard-bop ensembles large and small. But he is far more than that. A composer of a number of now-standard jazz tunes, he is also an excellent soloist and a fine leader in his own right.

Born in 1934 in Dallas, Texas, Walton studied piano with his mother. He attended the University of Denver and moved to New York in 1955 to be a musician. The U.S. Army had other ideas, and he was stationed in Germany, where he played with such musicians as Eddie Harris, Don Ellis, and Leo Wright. Walton moved back to New York after he got out of the Army, and quickly became part of the professional jazz scene, playing with Kenny Dorham, Lou Donaldson, Gigi Gryce, J.J. Johnson and the Art Farmer/Benny Golson Jazztet. But his real breakthrough came when he became the pianist in Art Blakey's Jazz Messengers, playing alongside Freddie Hubbard and Wayne Shorter. Walton's tunes became part of the Blakey repertoire, and such tunes as "Bolivia" and "Firm Roots" are now jazz repertoire classics.

After leaving Blakey, he became musical director for Abbey Lincoln and continued to be featured with the top jazz artists of the day, Hank Mobley and Lee Morgan among them. In the '70s he formed Eastern Rebellion, recording a number of now-classic albums and touring. He continues to lead his own bands, serve as pianist in all-star groups, and record prolifically; an album as arranger/pianist for Etta James, *Mystery Lady*, won a Grammy Award.

D I S C O G R A P H Y

Bolivia - Eastern Rebellion - LP: Timeless SJP 101 (+CD)

Bremond's Blues - Ironclad: Live at Yoshi's - CD: Monarch MR1005

Firm Roots - Eastern Rebellion 2 - LP: Timeless SJP 106 (+CD)

I'm Old Fashioned, The Meaning of the Blues, Stella by Starlight - Live at Maybeck Recital Hall Series Vol. 25 - CD: Concord Jazz CCD 4546

If I Were a Bell - Ray Brown/Milt Jackson Quartet: It Don't Mean a Thing if You Can't Pat Your Foot to It - LP: Pablo 2310-909; CD: OJC-601

Something in Common - Cedar Walton Plays - CD: Delos D/CD4008

BOLIVIA

By CEDAR WALTON

George Coleman's Solo
4 Choruses

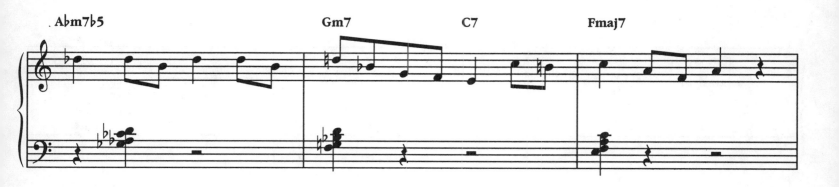

10

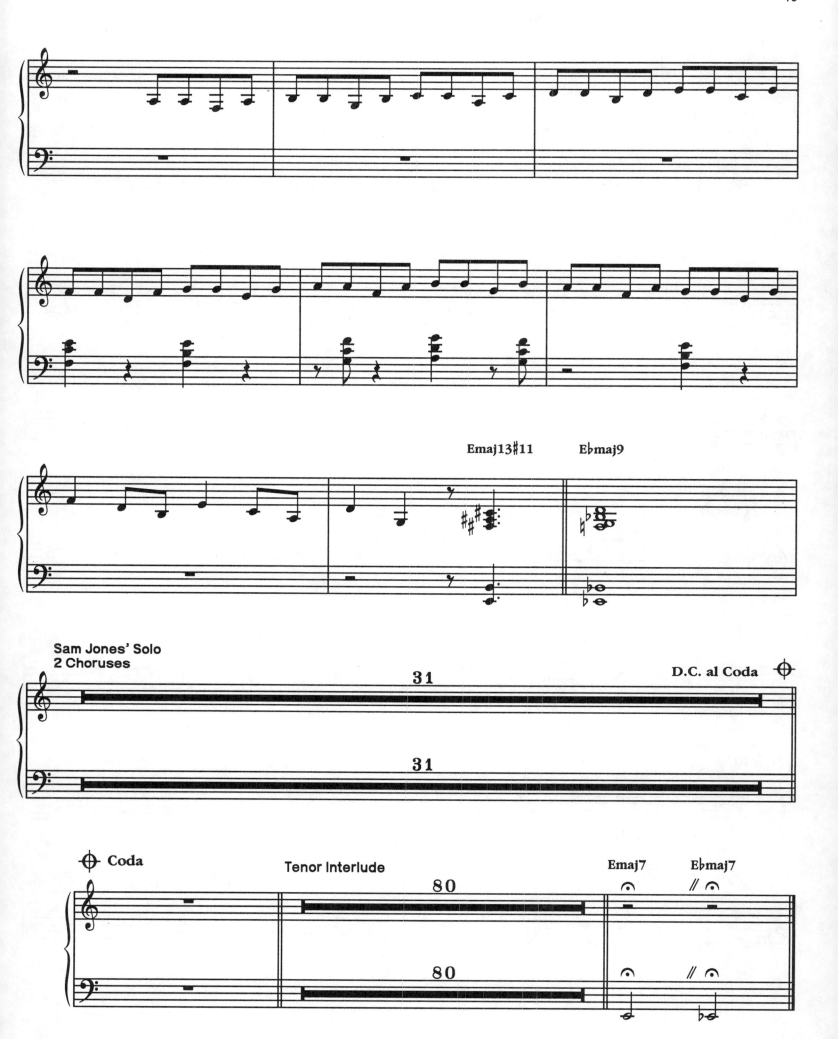

BREMOND'S BLUES

By CEDAR WALTON

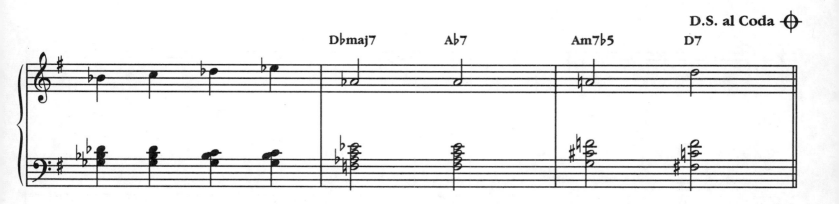

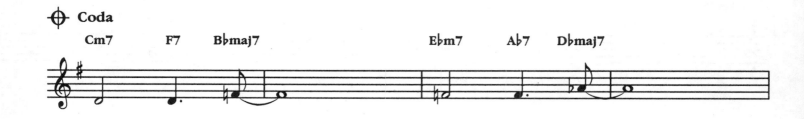

IF I WERE A BELL

from GUYS AND DOLLS

By FRANK LOESSER

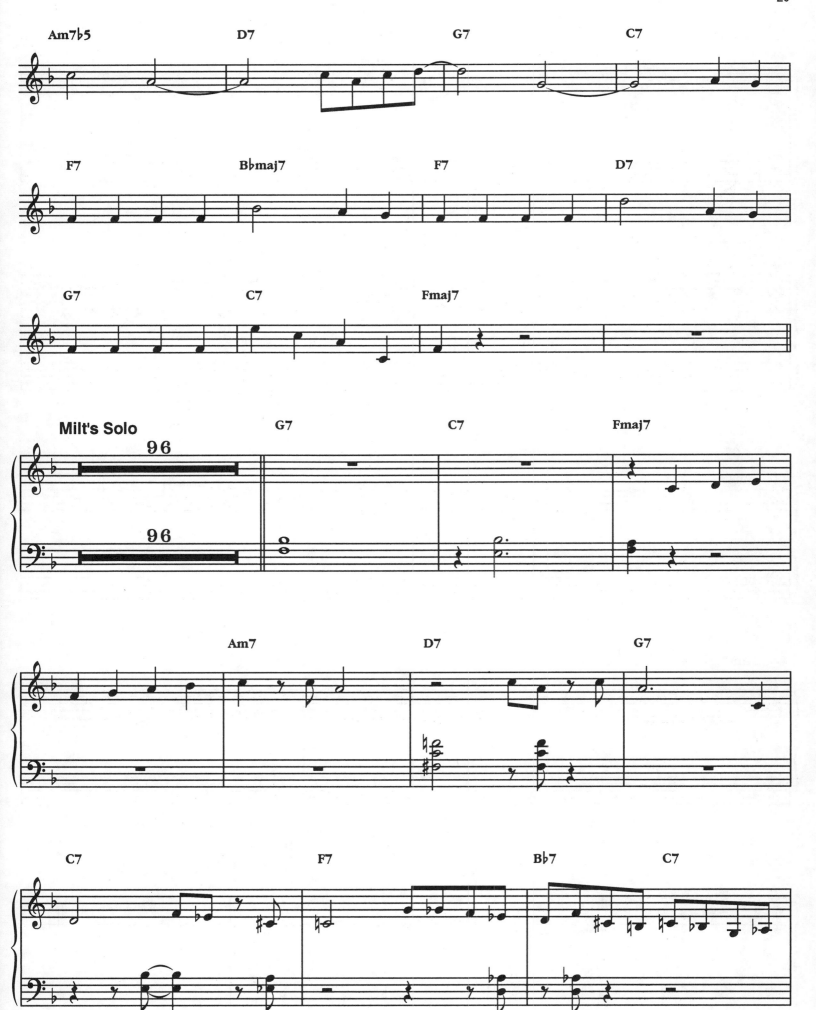

FIRM ROOTS

By CEDAR WALTON

Intro

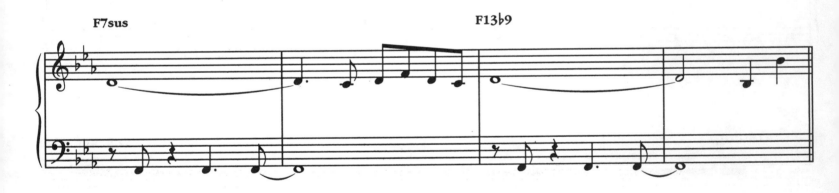

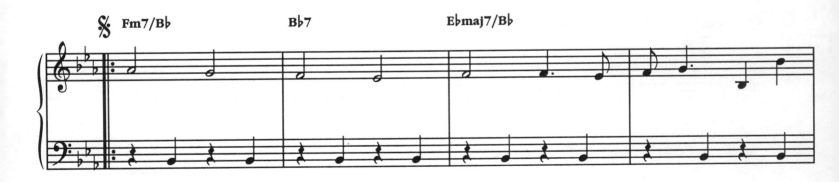

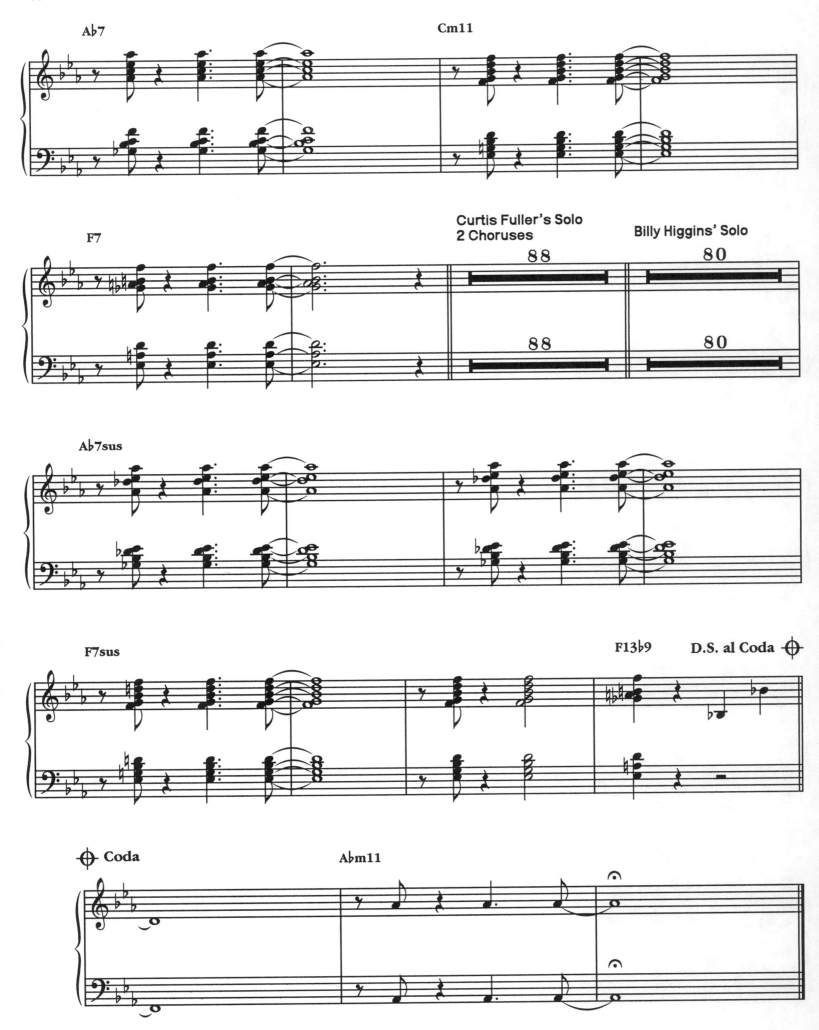

I'M OLD FASHIONED

from YOU WERE NEVER LOVELIER

Words by JOHNNY MERCER
Music by JEROME KERN

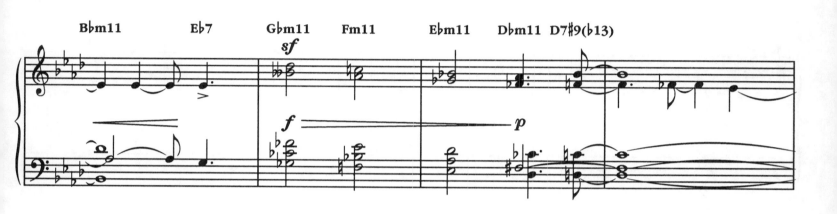

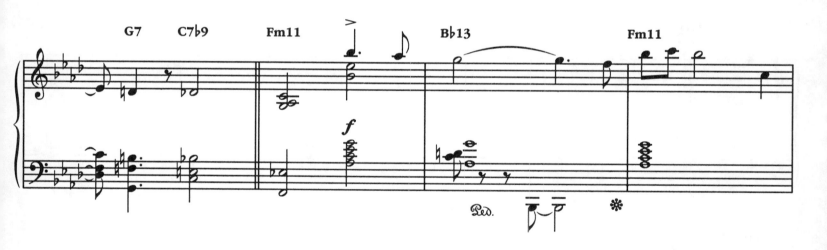

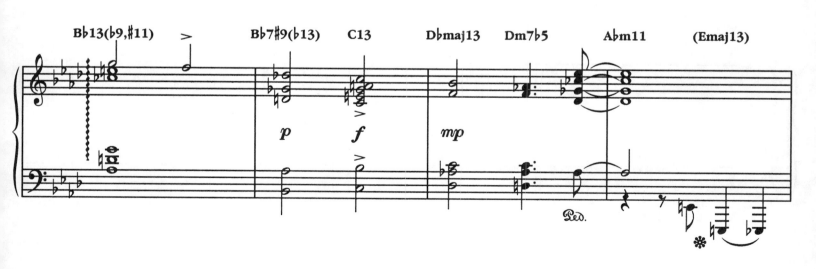

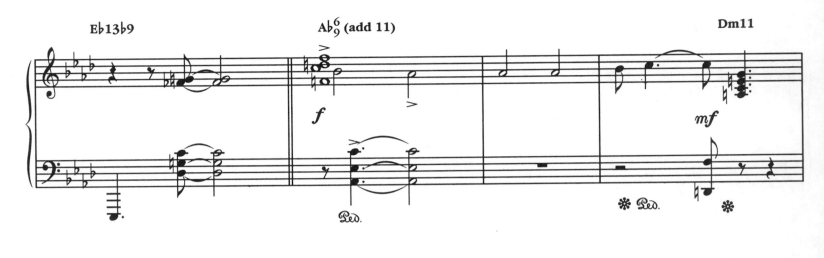

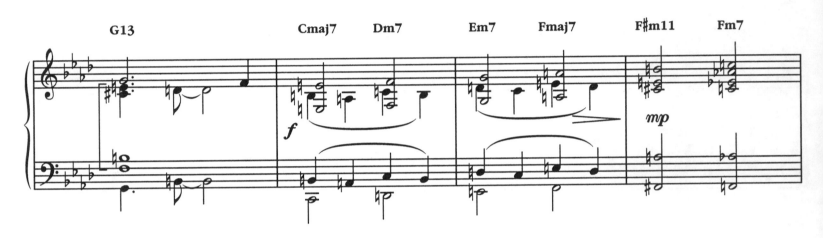

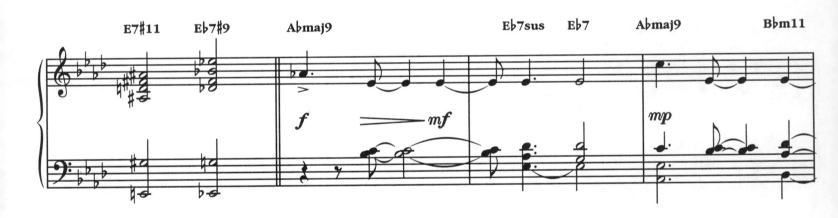

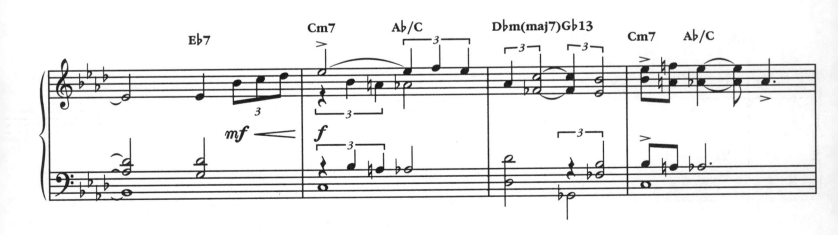

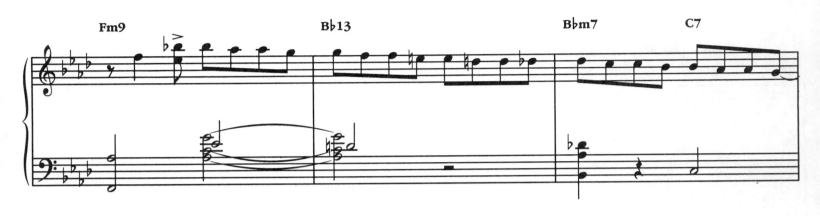

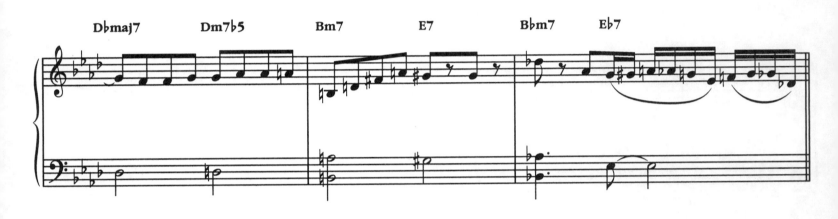

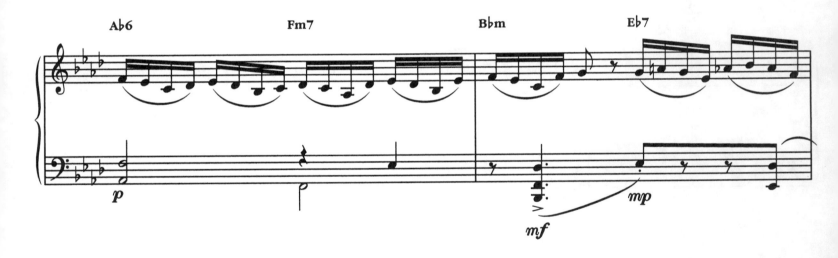

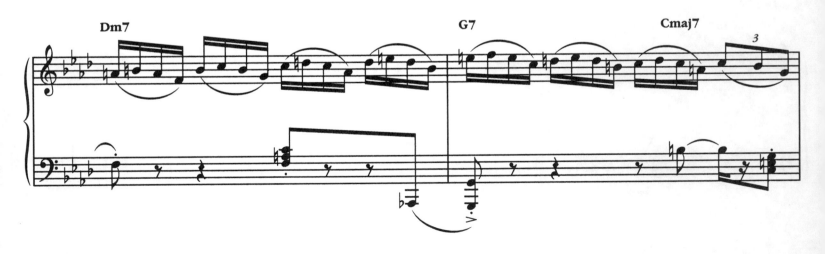

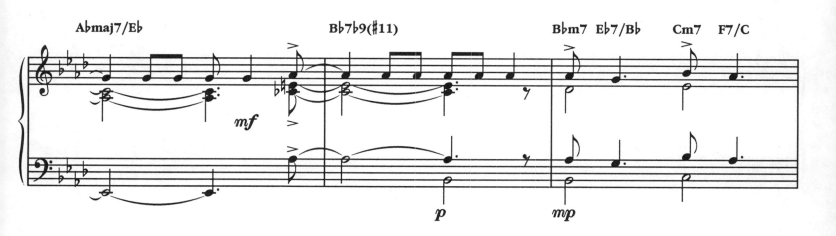

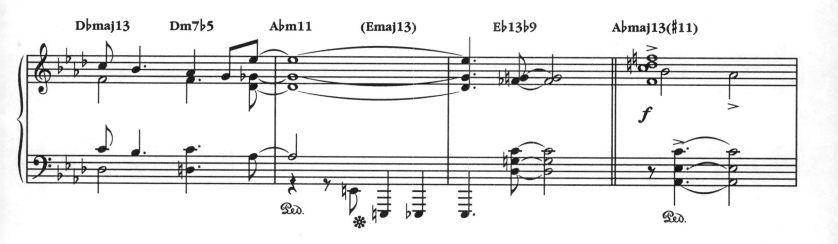

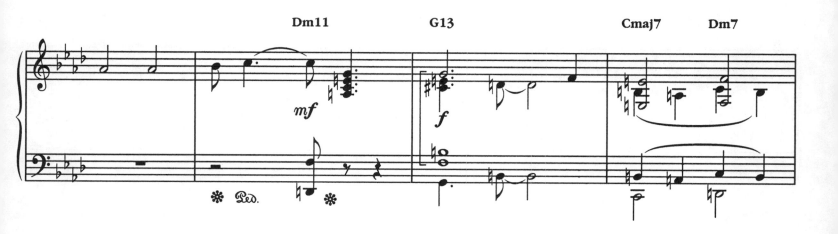

54

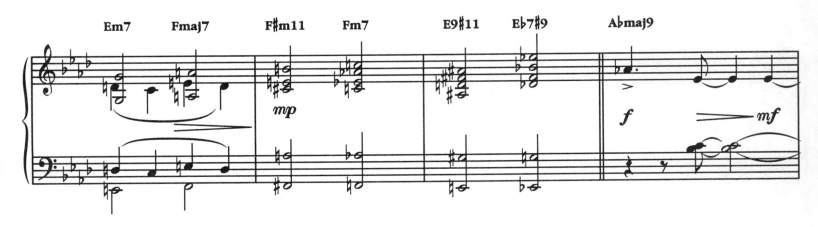

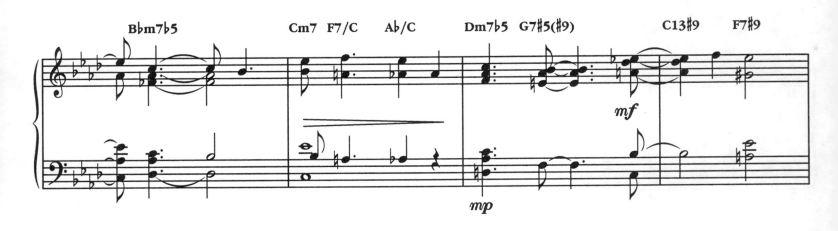

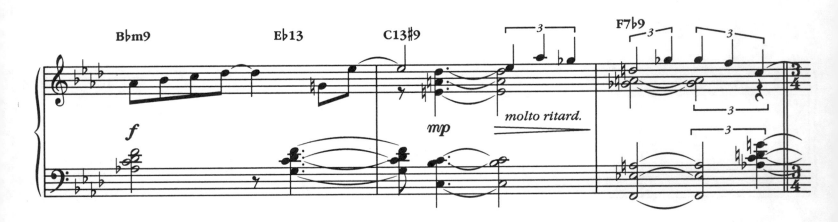

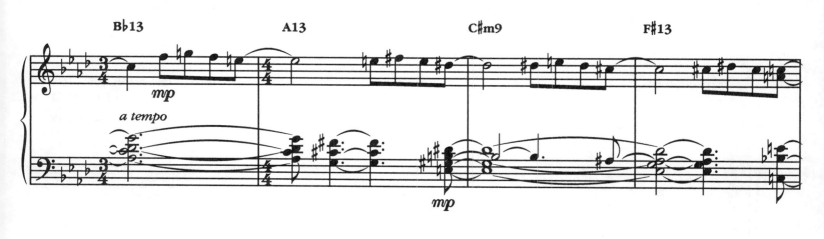

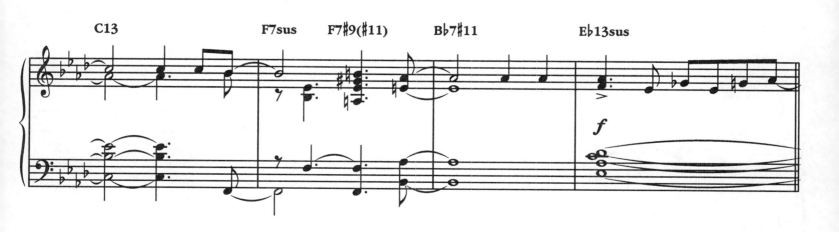

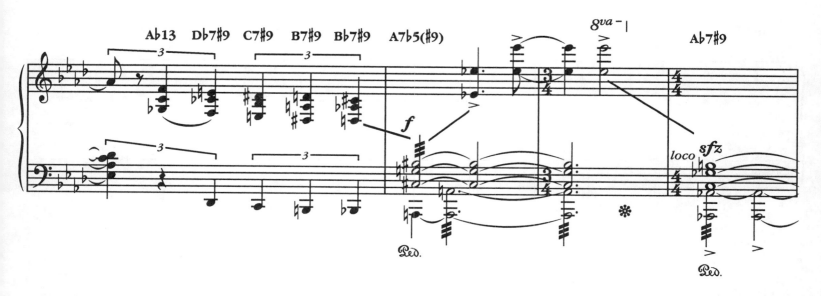

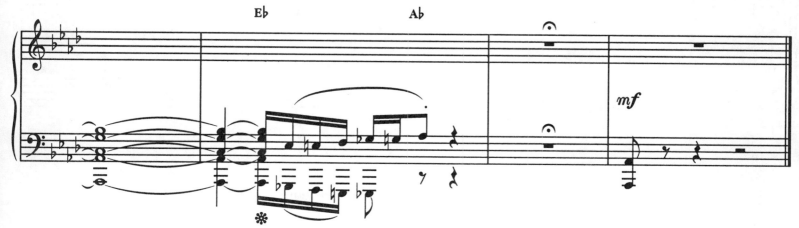

THE MEANING OF THE BLUES

Slow Swing

Words and Music by BOBBY TROUP
and LEAH WORTH

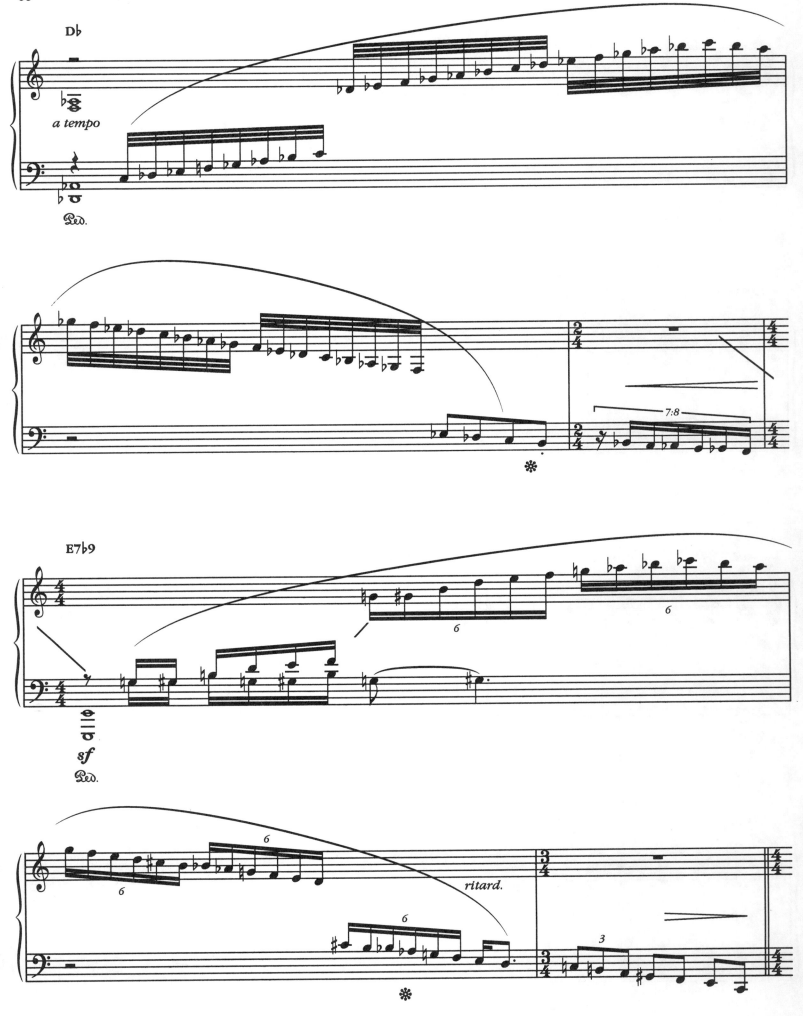

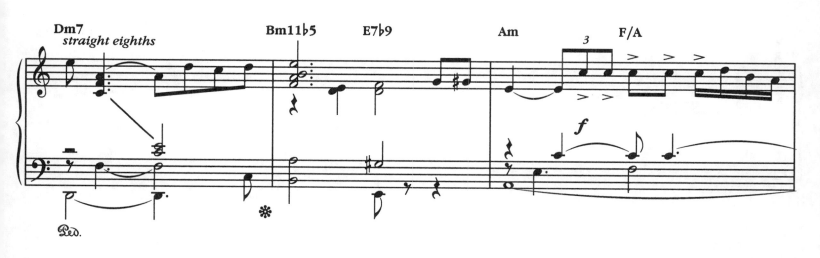

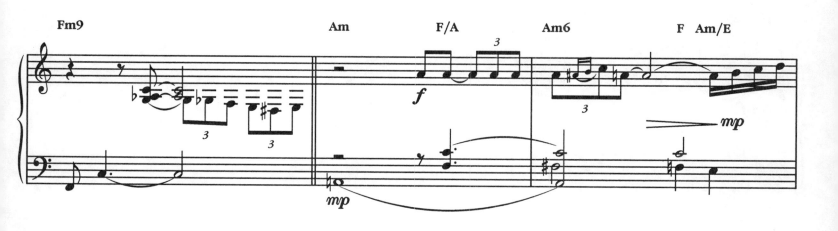

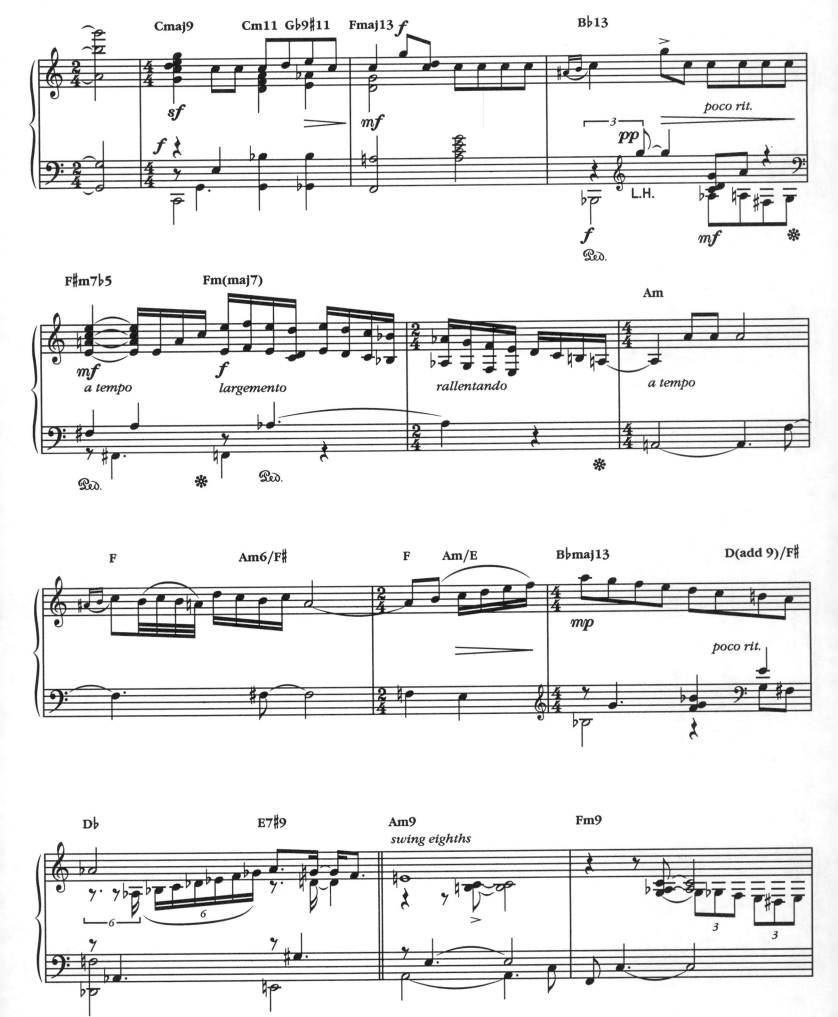

SOMETHING IN COMMON

By CEDAR WALTON

66

69

Ron Carter's Bass Solo

Interlude 3X

Last Time
D.S. al Coda

Coda

STELLA BY STARLIGHT

from the Paramount Picture THE UNINVITED

Words by NED WASHINGTON
Music by VICTOR YOUNG

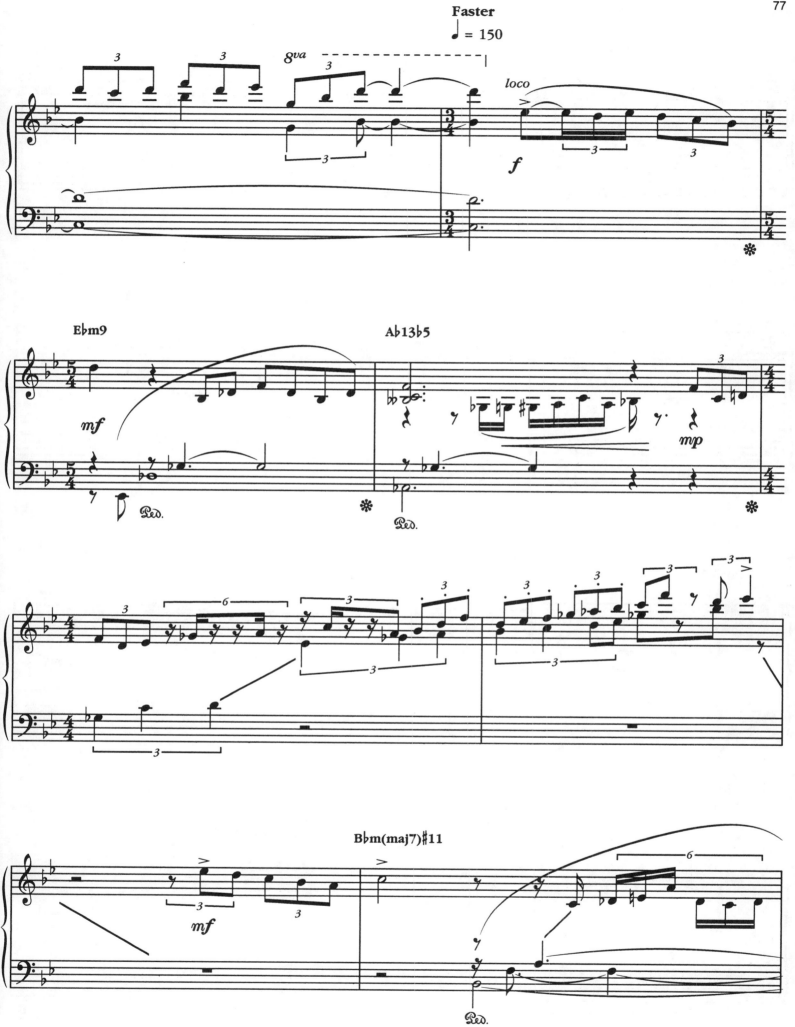

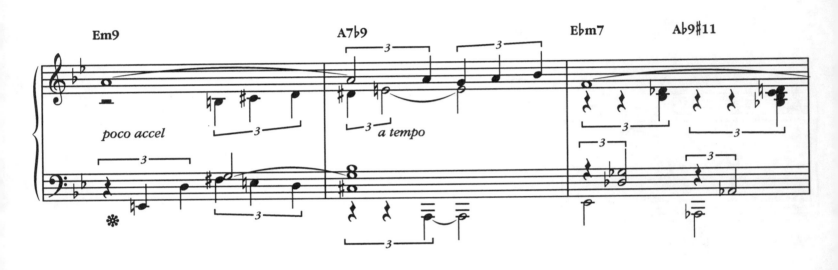

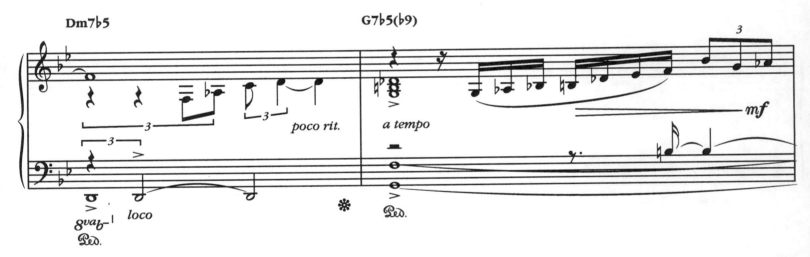

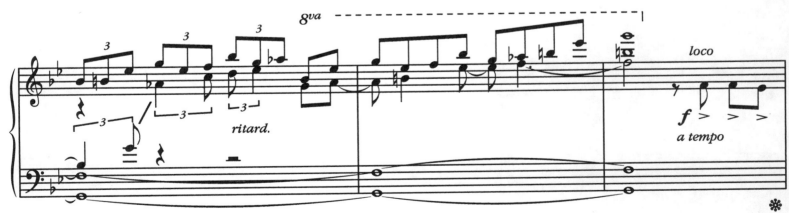

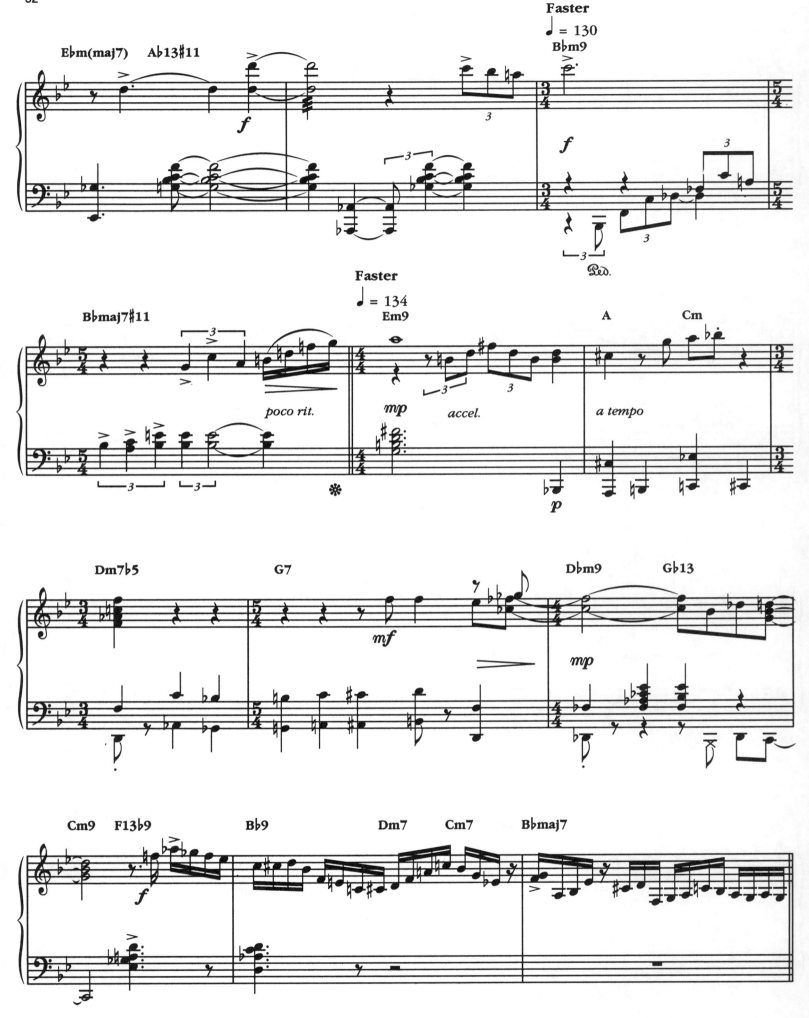

83

88

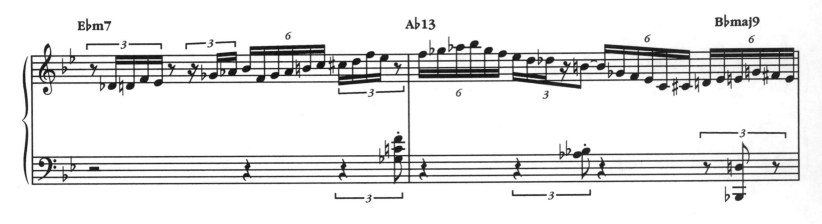

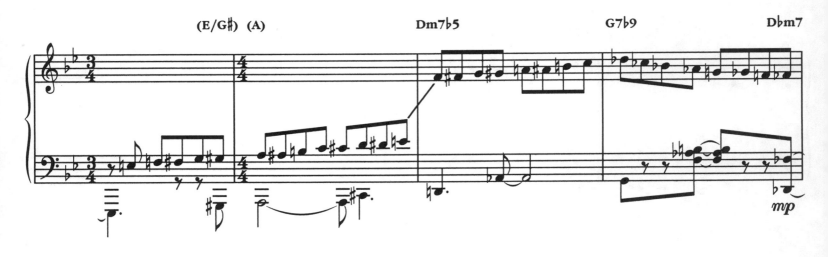

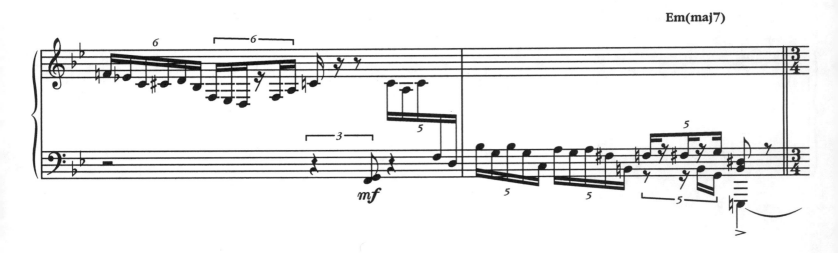

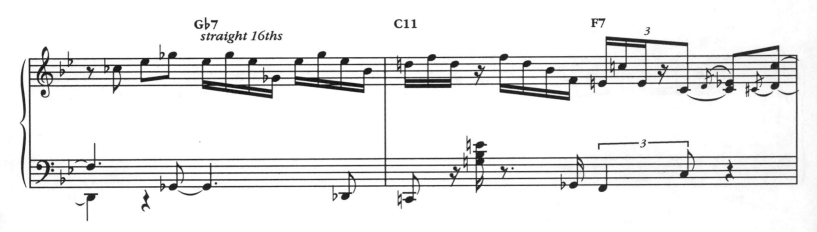

Quasi rubato

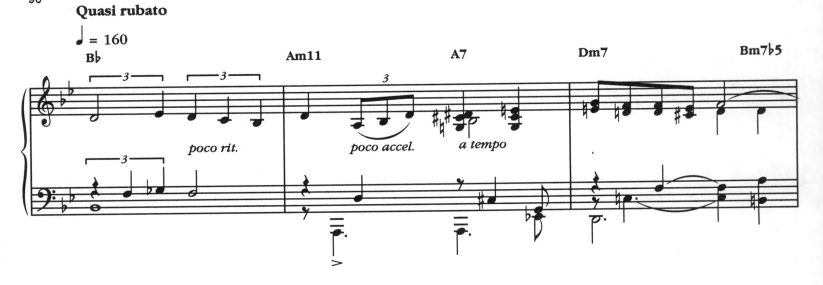

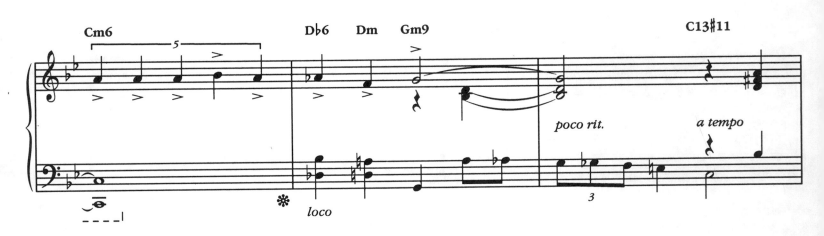

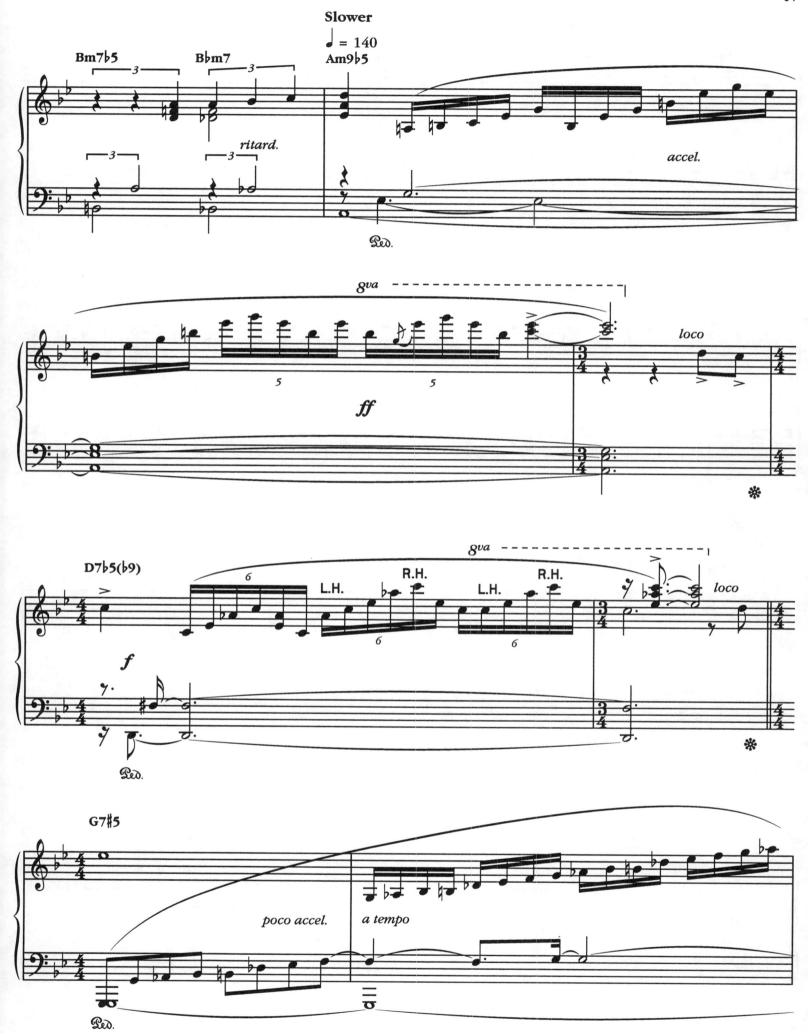

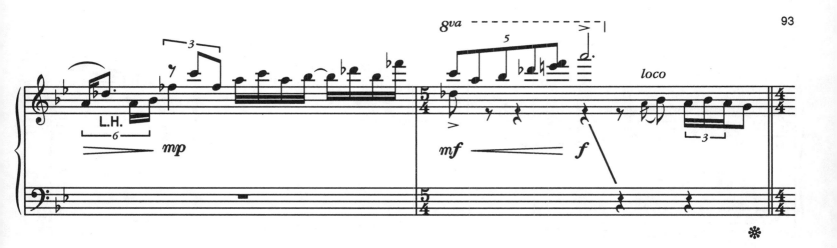

Moving

♩ = 146

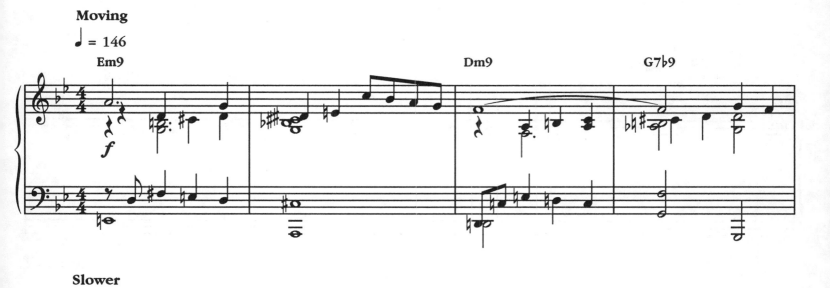

Slower

♩ = 130

a little slower

♩ = 120

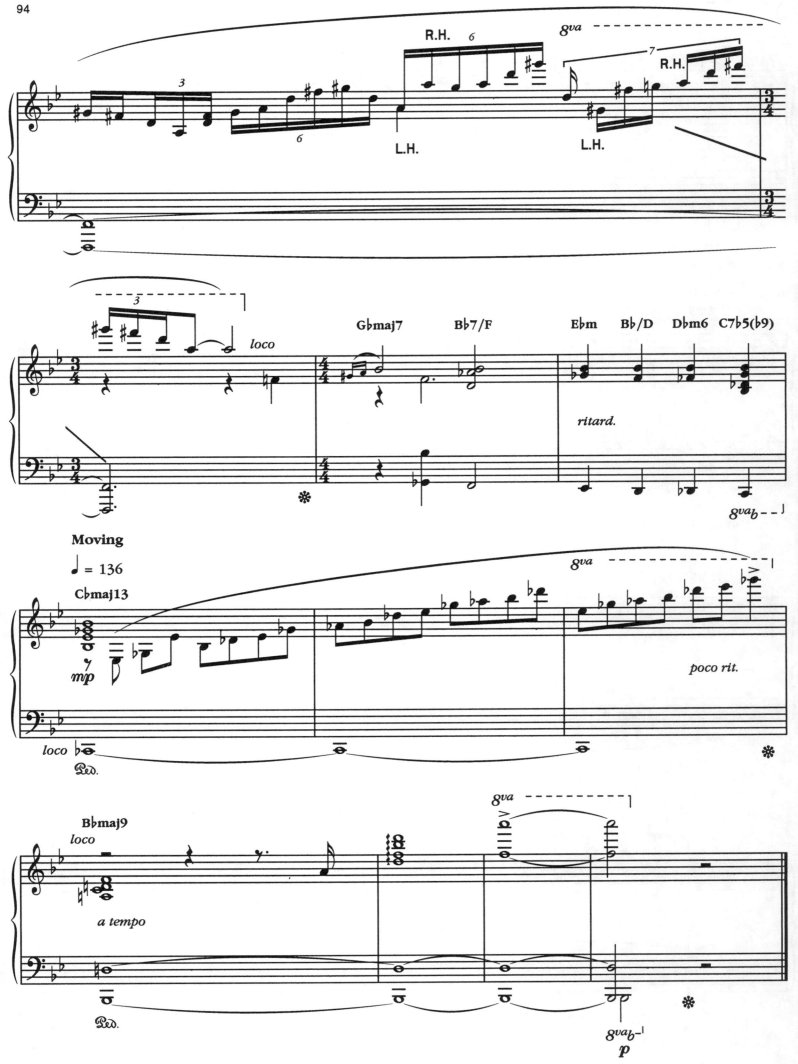

THE HAL LEONARD
REAL JAZZ BOOK

CHECK OUT THESE GREAT FEATURES!

- *Terrific songs in styles including standards, bebop, Latin, fusion & more!*

- *Lots of original material associated with major artists*

- *Hard-to-find modern jazz repertoire*

- *Many songs appearing in print for the first time ever!*

- *Lyrics are included if they exist for a tune*

- *Easy-to-read music typography*

- *A songwriter index for reference*

OUTSTANDING JAZZ ARTISTS REPRESENTED INCLUDE:

Louis Armstrong • Count Basie • Bix Beiderbecke • Dave Brubeck • Billy Childs • Nat King Cole • John Coltrane • Chick Corea • Miles Davis • Al DiMeola • Billy Eckstine • Duke Ellington • Peter Erskine • Kevin Eubanks • Bill Evans • Ella Fitzgerald • Dizzy Gillespie • Benny Green • Dave Grusin • Herbie Hancock • Coleman Hawkins • Billie Holiday • Dick Hyman • Al Jarreau • Antonio Carlos Jobim • Thad Jones • Abbey Lincoln • Joe Lovano • Chuck Magione • Pat Metheny • Charles Mingus • Thelonious Monk • Jelly Roll Morton • Gerry Mulligan • Oliver Nelson • Charlie Parker • John Patitucci • Art Pepper • Oscar Peterson • Bud Powell • Django Reinhardt • The Rippingtons • Sonny Rollins • Horace Silver • Spyro Gyra • Steely Dan • Mike Stern • Art Tatum • McCoy Tyner • Sarah Vaughan • Fats Waller • Weather Report

AND MANY MORE JAZZ GREATS!

OVER 500 SONGS, INCLUDING THESE GREAT STANDARDS:

Alfie • Alice in Wonderland • April in Paris • Autumn in New York • Besame Mucho • Black Coffee • Brazil • Caravan • Cast Your Fate to the Wind • Don't Worry 'Bout Me • (Meet) The Flintstones • Georgia on My Mind • Girl Talk • Gravy Waltz • How Deep Is the Ocean • I Wished on the Moon • I Got the World on a String • In a Sentimental Mood • In the Wee Small Hours of the Morning • Isn't It Romantic? • Jitterbug Waltz • Lover • Makin' Whoopee! • Mission: Impossible Theme • Mood Indigo • My Old Flame • Norwegian Wood • Out of Nowhere • The Rainbow Connection • The Shadow of Your Smile • Somebody Loves Me • Sophisticated Lady • Star Dust • Stella by Starlight • Take Five • Tangerine • This Masquerade • Too Late Now • The Very Thought of You • Watermelon Man • Wave • When Sunny Gets Blue • hundreds more!